CELTIC
for the Rhythm of Each Day
PRAYERS

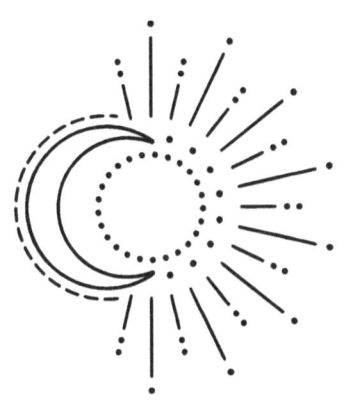

CELTIC PRAYERS

for the Rhythm of Each Day

RAY SIMPSON

Copyright © Ray Simpson, 2022.

All rights reserved. This book or any portion thereof may not be reproduced or used in any manner whatsoever without the express written permission of the publisher except for the use of brief quotations.

Anamchara Books
Vestal, New York 13850
www.AnamcharaBooks.com

Paperback ISBN: 978-1-62524-846-6
eBook ISBN: 978-1-62524-847-3

Cover design by Ellyn Sanna.
Sun & moon icons by Biancaoddi (Dreamstime).

CONTENTS

INTRODUCTION	9
WAKING UP	13
AT THE START OF THE WORKDAY	35
MIDDAY	57
AT THE END OF THE WORKDAY	79
EVENING	101
BEDTIME	123
IN THE MIDDLE OF THE NIGHT	145

God with me rising up;

God with me working.

God with me sharing meals;

God with me lying down.

Christ with me sleeping;

Christ with me waking.

In the rhythm of each day,

Spirit with me now;

Spirit with me evermore.

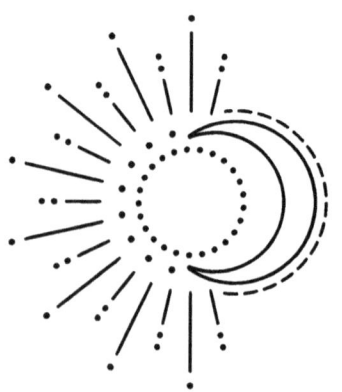

Introduction

More than two thousand years ago, the psalmist wrote, "Seven times a day I praise you" (Psalm 119:164). The early followers of Christ continued the ancient Jewish tradition of prayer throughout the day, but their prayers followed the flow of the Roman workday: bells began the workday at six in the morning, sounded a mid-morning break at nine, rang again for the noon meal and siesta, announced the recommencing of trade at three in the afternoon, and closed the business day at six. Christ's followers transformed this daily work schedule into a structure for prayer.

The ancient Celtic Christians also used the rhythm of the day as a prayer pattern. Their daily prayers affirmed that God is present in the most ordinary moments: getting up in the morning, washing, working, eating, going to bed. Prayer shaped their consciousness, so that they became ever more aware that the Kingdom of Heaven is a constant and present reality, hidden within the veil of everyday life.

This book is a tool that helps us to follow their example, pausing throughout the day to connect with God, sanctifying the ordinary rhythms of the modern work week:

waking up
going to work
breaking for lunch
ending the workday
the evening hours
going to bed

Ray Simpson has given us twenty original prayers, written in the Celtic tradition or patterned after ancient Celtic prayers, for each of these moments of the workday. As we use these brief prayers to fill tiny pauses in our day with renewed awareness, we create a pattern of daily prayer.

As this pattern becomes habit, it creates a sturdy framework that holds steady throughout each day our connection with the Life-Giver. Each day's cycle becomes a sign of the Divine Presence in our lives, and the turning hours remind us to see God everywhere. At the same time, these prayers remind us to participate in the Life and Love that flow to us and through us.

This book can be used in a variety of ways. For example, you may want to pray the same morning prayer day after day until you feel ready to move on—or you may want to work your way through the prayers, praying a different one each day of the month. You could pray the same prayers for a week at a time, allowing each to sink deeply into your heart and mind before you move on to the next one.

If the thought of praying six times a day seems overwhelming, you may want to start with only a morning prayer and a bedtime prayer, and then, when that prayer rhythm becomes comfortable, add in a lunchtime prayer. You might then use your morning commute as an opportunity to offer the day ahead to God, while your evening commute could be at time to reconnect with the Divine, a holy pause between the pressures of the workday and the responsibilities of the evening. A time of evening prayer may be the most difficult to fit into your busy schedule; some days you may find a moment, some days you may not. These prayers only require a few minutes—but it's okay to be flexible!

It's all too easy to miss the Divine revelations that punctuate our lives. After all, our culture constantly directs our attention elsewhere. We live our lives focused on our endless to-do lists, preoccupied with the past and future, rather than being truly present in the ordinary reality of the right-now, the sacred moment that connects us to eternity. We set boundaries in time and space around our "holy times," restricting them, perhaps, to Sunday mornings inside a church.

This book calls us to set prayer free, allowing it to flow out through the hours of every workday. As Jesus says in the Gospel of Thomas, "Split a piece of wood, and I am there. Lift up the stone, and you will find me there." In today's world, he might have said, "Start your car, and I am there. Turn on your computer, and you will find me there."

Like generations of earlier followers of Christ, we too can bless the rhythm of our daily lives. We can steep our days in prayer, infusing the hours with an awareness of God. The same Spirit who blew through ancient days still breathes in the hours of our modern life.

Every hour is holy, every day is sacred.

— Ellyn Sanna

Anamchara Books

waking up

1

I arise today in the fullness of my humanity.

I arise today in the glory of creation.

I arise today in the strength of the living God.

I arise today in gratitude.

I arise today in forgiveness.

I arise today in eagerness.

I arise today in the power of the great Creator
who brings me into being.

I arise today in the power of the great Son
who surmounts the things that shrink my being.

I arise today in the power of the great Spirit
who enables me to grow.

2

Life-giving God, the world lies open before you

and you summon the day to dawn.

Open my being,

and I shall show life.

Open my heart,

and I shall show love.

Open my mouth,

and I shall speak praise.

3

Creator of light,

at the rising of your sun

I rise to greet you,

meet you,

and reflect your light on earth.

When I wake up

may I feel the sun is shining on me

because you are smiling down on me.

Chase away dark thoughts.

Make me smile.

4

Make whole the leisure and activity of this day.

Restrain its hostile impulses,

fill all its moments with your love.

Come, Creator Spirit,

fresh as the morning dew.

Revive me and make me new.

5

I arise today

in the joy of being alive,

in the freedom of God's Spirit,

in the eagerness of service.

I arise today

in the wisdom of the One

who brought to birth the mountains,

the water, and the first beings.

6

I arise today

in the brilliance of the sun:

its fire to warm me,

its beams to light me,

its rays to cheer me.

I arise today

in the power of the Sun of suns:

the Sun of truth,

the Sun of life,

the Sun without end.

7

I arise today

in the Eternal Flow of Mercy

who was here when the land began to breathe,

when the Earth first grew green,

and when the first tribes began to roam.

I arise today

in the eternal Flow of Wisdom

who is perceived in the stones,

the stories, and the studies of all peoples.

I arise today

in the eternal Flow of Life

who seeps through land and limb and love.

8

I arise today,

the sun to encircle me,

the Earth to uphold me,

the air to enfold me.

I arise today,

God's way to uphold me,

God's gifts to equip me,

God's love to inspire me.

9

I arise today in the goodness of creation.
I arise today in the green life of the fertile ground.
I arise today in the promise of the seed.

Awaken me to your glory,
stir me to adventure,
restore my seeing,
cure my deafness,
heal my hardness,
and steer me toward my destiny.

10

God of life, you summon the day to dawn
and call me to create with you.
You are the Rock from which all earth is fashioned.
You are the Food from which all souls are fed.
You are the Force from which all power lines travel.
You are the Source who is creation's fountainhead.
You are the Heart from which all hearts are beating.
You are the Mind from which
come thoughts and dreams.
You are the Eye from which comes all my seeing.
You are the Gift from whom all mercy streams.
You are the Ache from which comes all my longing.
You are the Pain in which I bear my grief.
You are the Wind by which all souls go winging.
You are the One from whom flows all my life.

11

I arise today

in the simplicity of the waiting soil,

in the strength of the fierce elements,

in the deep formation of winter.

Stripped of inessentials, I stand, rooted in you,

in the anticipation of gathering strength,

for you sustain my well-being.

In the humility of the bare earth,

I welcome you:

Do your work in me.

12

I arise today

through the strength of Christ's life.

I arise today

through the humility of Christ's

crucifixion and burial.

I arise today

through the victory

of his resurrection and ascension.

I arise today

through the energy of the sun,

the willingness of rivers,

the joy of beasts, the song of birds,

and the love that makes the world.

13

Living One, I don't feel very alive this morning,

but I thank you for the gift of life.

I don't look forward to this day,

but I thank you for the gift of today.

You are.

I am.

We'll be.

14

As I arise from sleep,
I consecrate this day to you.
I believe, O God of all gods,
that you are the eternal Creator of life.
I believe, O God of all peoples,
that you are the eternal Creator of love.
I believe you create earth and seas and skies.
I believe you create me in your image
and give me eternal worth.
I honor you with my whole being
and consecrate this day to you.

15

Good morning, God.
My moans and groans I give now to you.
Today, may your glory be seen in me
as I become fully alive, warts and all.
Life of Being, flow through me now.

May I do this day on earth
as the saints do in heaven.
May I live this day in your light
and walk in the hope of your kingdom.

16

I arise today in the strength of the Birther

who brought me to life.

The Spirit will birth

a million wondrous miracles today,

composing the songs of the birds

and the buzz of the bees,

the laughter of children,

and the conversations between friends.

I ask of you just one more miracle, Spirit of Love:

Beautify my soul

throughout this day that you have made.

17

God bless the earth beneath me,
the sky above me,
the day before me,
your image deep within me.

Glory to you, Christ my King,
radiant with light,
the Sun who shines on all the world.
Earth, exalt! Heaven, rejoice!
At morning light, I give you thanks and praise!

18

When I awake in weakness,

turn my eyes to the Presence.

When in gloom I arise,

bring light to my soul,

even as you bring light to the Earth.

19

O loving Christ, hanged on a tree
yet risen in the morning,
as the sun dispels the mist from the hills.
scatter the darkness from my soul.

20

I give you thanks, Great Spirit,
for the sun,
and for the warmth that penetrates
through trunks of trees,
through mists, through walls,
warming caves and corridors.
As you wake me for this day,
in my mind may it too be so.

At the start of the workday

1

As I begin my workday, God,

I come to you.

Bless to me my body.

Bless to me my soul.

Bless to me my living.

Bless to me my goals.

2

Life-Giver,

circle this building in which I work each day,

and keep destructive things without:

lack of self-esteem,

confusion,

prejudice,

pride,

bullying,

cheating,

shame,

malicious gossip.

Life-Giver, circle this building,

and keep all that is good and true within.

3

Be with me today, Life Giver,

    in my meetings,

    in my temptations,

    in my loneliness.

Be with me today, Life-Giver,

    in the humdrum,

    in the opportunities,

    in the possibilities.

4

We weave this day, Spirit:

silence of knowing,

clearness of seeing,

grace of speaking.

We weave this day, Spirit:

humility of listening,

depth of understanding,

joy of serving.

We weave this day, Sprit:

peace of being,

gift of loving,

power of meeting.

5

Glad Bringer of brightness,

day's blessing, rainbow's embrace,

teach my heart to open like a blossom

to welcome in your grace.

Teach me to dance with the trees in the wind

and to laugh with the sun's smile on my face.

The Earth is yours; may it bring forth its produce.

The birds are yours; may they bring forth their songs.

My work is yours; may it bring forth its yield.

6

Teach me, dear God,

to know you better,

explore your world,

learn from mistakes,

understand others,

use my talents,

remember important things,

and grow like Jesus.

7

Lord, I offer you all I am,
all I have, all I do,
and all whom I shall meet this day,
that you will be given the glory.
I offer you our homes and work,
our schools and leisure,
and everyone in our community today;
may all be done as if for you.
I offer you the broken and hungry.
May the wealth and work of the world
be available to all and exploited by none.
May your presence be known to all.

8

Dear Jesus,

a good voice speaks within me.

and a destructive voice also speaks.

Help me this day

to listen to the good voice,

who brings to me the wisdom of your Spirit,

and shut my ears to the destructive voice.

9

Teach me to dance like clouds that play.

Teach me to laugh like sun that glistens.

Teach me to flow like streams that sing.

Teach me to fly like birds on the wing.

Teach me to dream like rainbows gleam.

Teach me even in the midst of work

to delight myself in you.

10

Bless my eyes—so I notice others.

Bless my heart—so I love others.

Bless my hands—so I help others.

Where there is hate, let me bring love.

Where there are quarrels, let me bring peace.

Where there is darkness, let me bring light.

11

Our Father in heaven,
your kingdom come, your will be done
on earth as it is in heaven.
Your kingdom come,
because I am honest and do not cheat,
because I am fair and do not steal,
because I listen and do not laugh at others,
because I am a friend and do not gossip,
because I love and do not hate,
because I share and do not grab.

12

I give you thanks, Life-Giver,

because Earth's life and fruitfulness flow from you

and all times and seasons reflect your love.

I give you thanks

because you created the world in love,

you redeemed the world through love,

and you maintain the world by your love.

As I begin my workday,

may my heart be always open to your love.

13

As I step into the day's busyness,
Life of Jesus, Sun of suns,
fill every part of me.
May life be in my speech
and sense in what I say.
Love of Jesus, Sun of suns,
fill every heart with love,
and give me love in what I do.
Traversing sea and road and field,
rays of Jesus be my shield.

14

Creator God,

as my workday begins,

the raw materials are yours,

the energy is yours, the skills are yours,

those I work with are yours.

Work is your gift.

Into your hands I place

my materials, my energies,

my skills, and my colleagues.

You are my reward.

Rising from death, today Christ greets his people.

Rising with all creation, I greet him in my work.

15

May this be a day of resurrection and refreshment
for families and single people,
for businesses and communities.
May our homes be places of hospitality and hope,
that we may know your risen presence
as we share ourselves
and enjoy the company of others.
May our work honor you
and bring joy to the people we encounter
and healing to the land.

16

On our world, Spirit,
may your love descend today.
On all who work,
may your love descend today.
Where there is strife, Spirit,
may your love descend today.
Where there is neglect, Spirit,
may your love descend today.
Where there is violence, Spirit,
may your love descend today.
Where there is division, Spirit,
may your love descend today.
On all the Earth, Spirit,
may your love descend today.

17

May the Three of limitless love
be in the eye of each one with whom I work,
and pour upon me more and more generously,
hour by hour, your creative love
that gives meaning to my work.

18

As I enter my workplace, remind me that

I come into the presence of the creating Father;

I come into the presence of the workaday Son;

I come into the presence of the renewing Spirit;

I come into the presence of the Three in One.

19

Creator God who mothers me with unending love,
may the reality of your kingdom come to our world.
May your will be done on earth, as it is in heaven.

> In my work, may your kingdom come.
> In my pleasures, your kingdom come.
> In our leaders, your kingdom come.
> In my gatherings, your kingdom come.
> On the roads, your kingdom come.
> On the internet, your kingdom come.
> In each thing I do this day,
> your kingdom come.

20

In each hour of my workday,
make me aware, Spirit of Life,
of the Eye that beholds me,
the Hand that holds me,
the Heart that loves me,
the Presence that enfolds me.

MIDDAY

1

Great Spirit, whose breath is felt in the soft breeze,

I seek your strength at noon.

May my co-workers and I

and the peoples of the world

work in dignity and in the beauty of the day.

Spirit, a thousand voices shout at me this day:

soundbites and slogans, images and screens,

conversations and traffic, newspapers and internet.

Help me to filter out

and turn away all that is not of you,

and to spot and hold close all that is of you.

2

Great Spirit,

at noonday, as I pause from my busyness,

I become aware once more of your Presence.

I remember your love that gave birth to the universe,

and that you put in place

all that is needed for growth.

You trusted us to care for and guard your creation.

Forgive our delusions of self-sufficiency

and our harming of the environment.

Forgive our taking food for granted

and our dishonoring of the farmer.

Restore us and restore the land.

As I return to my work, may I be your hands,

working to heal the wounds I too have dealt

your creation.

3

As I return to work,
may I see the face of Christ
in everyone I meet.
May everyone I meet
see the face of Christ in me

Holy Spirit, refine me,
that I may be just and true.
Sending Spirit, release me
from anything that holds me back,
that I may touch lives for you.
Disturbing Spirit, recharge me,
so I don't settle for the status quo.

4

When the day is drab,

come, Holy Spirit.

When my heart harbors fear,

come, Holy Spirit.

When my life is like parched land,

come, Holy Spirit, with fresh hope to strengthen me.

I thank you for time to pause at midday,

and I pray that you renew my mind.

Birther of the human race,

you summon me and call me to live in communion.

5

Stop!

It's the middle of the day.

Time to recognize:

I get too full of myself.

I get upset too easily.

I want things to go my way.

Please, God,

use this lunch hour

to calm me down.

6

As I step away from my duties,

Wind of Heaven,

blow away dross and deceits;

refresh my battered soul;

brace me for what is to come.

Blow through me now as I return to work.

Give me a clean heart and a focused mind,

so that whatever work I do,

I do it unto you.

7

Holy Spirit,

come as a gentle breeze

that cools the noonday heat.

Come as the calming Presence

that restores stillness to my being.

Rest like dew on the violence of our world,

cooling tempers, humbling arrogance,

soothing division.

Rest like dew on my own heart

and on all I still have to do this day.

8

As the press of work pauses at noon,

may God's Rest be upon me.

As the sun rides high at noon,

may the Sun of Righteousness shine upon me.

As the rain refreshes the stained, stale streets,

may the Spirit bring rain upon my dry ground.

9

As I pause to think of you
in the midst of the busy day,
lead me from death to life,
and from falsehood to truth.
Lead me from despair to hope,
and from fear to trust.
Lead me from hate to love,
and from war to peace.
Deep peace of the Son of peace,
fill my heart, my workplace, my world.

10

Bless me now, Spirit, in the middle of the day.

Be with me and all who are dear to me

Teach me to follow the pattern

of your beautiful attitudes,

joyful, simple, and gentle.

Great Creator who never ceases to create,

you give me well-being in the midst of the day:

this is a day of renewal,

this is a day of growth,

this is a day of sharing food,

and this is a day for your love.

11

Great Spirit,

whose breath is felt in the soft breeze

even as your life surges through socket and screen,

I seek your strength in the middle of the day.

May I and all the peoples of the world

work in dignity

and walk in the beauty of the day.

12

O God, you called all life into being;

your presence is around me now;

your Spirit enlivens all who work.

May your kingdom come on earth.

Impart to me wisdom to understand your ways,

to manage well the tasks

that remain for me to do this day.

Make me a co-creator with you,

so that when the workday ends,

I may come to you without shame.

13

Good God, be with me
through the remainder of this day.
When I neglect you
remind me of your presence;
when I am frightened
give me courage;
when I am tempted
give me the power to resist;
when I am anxious and worried
give me peace;
when I am weary in service
renew my tired frame.

14

In the whirling wheels of the busy world,

you are with me, Spirit.

When the workday takes its toll,

you are with me.

In the clamor of strife,

you are with me.

When the world turns sour,

you are with me.

You birth in me renewed strength,

revived hope, fresh ideas,

a deeper calm, and the joy that comes from you.

15

Circle me, O God,

for the remainder of the day.

keep harm without,

keep good within.

May the eternal Glory shine upon me.

May the Son of Mary stay beside me.

May the life-giving Spirit be a canopy over me.

May the eternal Three be ever with me.

16

God of justice, God of peace,

in the heat of the day

I take refuge in you.

In the middle of the day

I remember you.

May I please you with my work.

May I please you with my words.

May I please you with my willingness

to love my neighbors

in every shape and form they come to me.

Even as I go back to work,

my heart kneels and adores you.

17

God of community,

Spirit of energy and change,

as I face the remainder of my day,

pour on me without reserve or distinction,

that this day, this hour, in this place,

I may have strength

to plant your justice on earth.

18

Lord Jesus, at this hour of the day
you hung on the cross,
stretching out your arms in love to all.
May the people of the world be
drawn to your uplifted love,
including those with whom I work this day.
Give me the will to share my bread with the hungry,
to give shelter to those who feel rejected,
and to reach out to those in need.
I pray especially
for those whose tasks are backbreaking,
whose bodies are mutilated,
or whose spirits are crushed.

19

Lord Jesus,

in the midst of mockery and madness

you found peace

to remain in your Father's will.

In the middle of the fretful day,

give me peace

to remain in your Spirit's will.

20

Renew me, O Risen Christ,

in the midst of the day.

In doubt, bring faith;

in disillusion, bring hope;

in cold indifference, bring tender mercy;

in shoddy expediency, bring untarnished ideals;

in the staleness of routine, bring new stirrings of life.

At the end of the workday

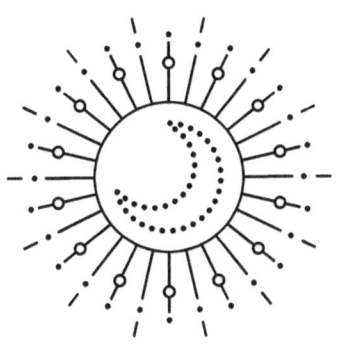

1

Let the light fade and the work be done.

As the flowers and the laptops close,

as the sun goes down and the busy world stills,

let the Son of God draw near.

Spirit of the Risen Christ,

as lamps light up the evening,

shine into my heart and kindle in me

the fire of your love.

2

As I put my work away,

I offer to you, Spirit of Peace,

the troubles of this day;

I lay down my burdens at your feet.

Forgive me my sins, give me your peace,

and help me this evening to receive your Word.

3

I give you thanks that you are always present,
> in all moments throughout each day.

I give you thanks for all I experienced today,
> even the things that challenged me.

I give you thanks for the blessings of this day,
and I ask your blessing on the night ahead.

4

As I leave my work behind,

may I let it rest in your hands.

The Creator who brought order out of chaos,

give peace to me.

The Savior who calmed the raging sea,

give peace to me.

The Spirit who broods upon the deeps,

give peace to me.

5

Creator God, my work is done for today.

I offer you this day's troubles;

help me to let them be until tomorrow.

And when tomorrow comes,

give me strength to bear them,

wisdom to handle them,

compassion for those who brought them,

peace as to their outcome.

6

As I ready myself to return to home and family,

illumine my heart, O Light-Giver;

implant in me a desire for your truth.

May all that is false within me flee.

May I walk in the hope of your kingdom.

Fill me with your light and love.

Be with me all through the evening that lies ahead,

Creator, Christ, and Holy Spirit.

Be in what I do, inform what I say,

shine through who I am.

7

Life-Giver, as we return from school and work,

keep these good things within:

forgiveness, patience,

a sense of wonder,

the warmth of companionship,

respect for all, service to others,

teamwork between children and adults,

care for the planet,

reverence for life,

fitness of body, mind, and spirit.

8

Perfect Comforter! Wonderful Refreshment!

You make peace dwell in my soul.

Now, as I end my daily labor,

you offer rest;

in weakness, strength;

in boredom, inspiration;

and in failure, new hope.

From heaven shine forth your glorious light

as I end this busy day.

9

As I end another workday,
you, Life-Giver are my strength;
you alone are sufficient.
Guardian, be over the restless people,
a covering of truth and peace;
be over the hopeless people,
a shelter of promise and potential;
be over the tired people,
a fresh shower of energy and calm.

10

O Being of life!

O Being of peace!

O Being of time!

Be with me as I end my workday.

O Being of truth!

O Being of sight!

O Being of wisdom!

Be with me as I end my workday.

11

Lord, you were tested by the evil one;

break in me the hold of power and pride.

You knew deep tears and weaknesses;

help me to be vulnerable for you.

You followed to the end the way of the cross;

help me to be faithful to you as I end this busy day—

and to the end of my days.

12

God of the call,

I pray for those who feel thwarted in their vocation.

I pray for those who are discouraged,

unemployed, or too sick to work.

God from whom all truth and justice flow,

I pray for your rule of love to prevail.

Banish prejudice and injustice from workplaces.

May I do on earth as the saints do in heaven.

God of resurrection,

may I bring honor to you,

joy to the people, and healing to the land.

May I do on earth as the saints do in heaven.

13

Thank you for your love for me,

strong and nurturing;

I give back my life to you.

Thank you for my mind and body;

I give back my life to you.

Thank you for the past day;

I give back my life to you.

After creation God rested and so may I;

I give back my life to you.

14

I thank you for your presence through this day

and for friends who have helped me on my way.

As the wheels of the world grow still,

forgive me for my failures in love.

Kindle in my heart, O Loving One,

the flame of the love that never ceases,

that it may burn in me through

the remainder of this day,

till I shine forever in your presence.

15

Give me sorrow for my sins
against human dignity and hospitality.
Give me sorrow for the sins of this day.
Renew in me your love,
so that I may face the evening
with humility and grace.

16

Healing Christ,

you walk the world with those who suffer

in broken places of the world.

Now, as this day's work is done,

I come to you with my wounds and theirs.

Encircle those for whom I pray.

Enter their bodies, minds, and spirits,

and heal them of all that harms.

17

Eternal Creator of the hours and days,

as this workday draws to a close,

draw close to me,

and may I draw close to you.

Eternal Creator of the hours and days,

as this day's work is done, draw near to me,

and may I draw near to you.

18

As the work is done,

may the Light of lights come to my shadowed heart;

may the Spirit's wisdom come to my clouded mind.

May the peace of the Spirit be mine this night,

the peace of the Son be mine this night,

the peace of the Father be mine this night,

the peace of all peace be mine this night.

Into your hands, O Living One,

I place my family, my neighbors,

my brothers and sisters in Christ,

and all whom I have met today:

enfold them in your will.

19

As the busy day grows still,

I sense you, my Maker;

I feel your hand upon me.

All that has been made

stirs within me creation's song of praise.

Now I give you thanks for work completed;

I give you thanks for the remainder of this day.

You created the world out of love.

Now I return to you in love.

20

As the workday is done,

in my tiredness be my Rest;

and where I stumbled be my Shield.

Into my place of darkness,

into my place of strife,

into my fears and worries,

come with eternal life.

EVENING

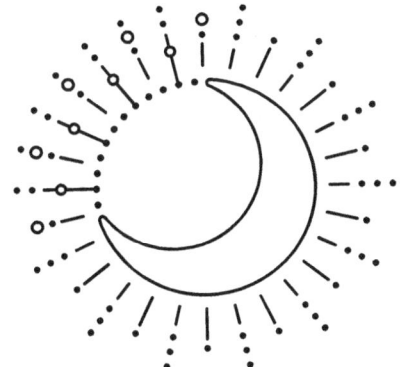

1

I come to you this evening,

the One who gives all life.

Use this time, at the end of the day,

to prepare me, like a samurai warrior,

for your next move.

May I move with you, attentive and supple,

alert to opportunities and pitfalls.

Keep me ready,

even in the evening of life,

that I may relish the coming privilege

of sitting at table with you and being served by you.

2

Into your hands, O Giver of Life,

I place all who are victims of prejudice,

oppression, or neglect;

the unwanted, the frail.

May everyone be cherished.

Into your hands, O Giver of Life,

I place all who are restless,

sick, or prey to the powers of evil.

Watch over them and watch over me this night.

Into your hands, O Giver of Life,

I place my family, my community, my nation—

and myself.

3

I bless you, O God,

and forget not all your benefits.

I bless you for your creation,

alive with your glory.

You nod and beckon to me

through every stone and star.

As the sun sets in the west,

may I settle down with you.

4

When we eat our evening meal,

may we think of the Earth who gives it.

When we get in a car,

may we think of the oil that moves it.

When we buy something in a store or online,

may we think of the people who made it.

As evening turns to night,

may we think of you who creates us.

5

As the sun sets in the west

calm my spirit, Spirit of Peace.

Into your hands I place

my failings and irritations.

In your presence I give thanks

for the blessings of this day.

May I prepare to lie down at one with you

so that I may rise up ready to do your will.

6

The peace of the Spirit be ours this night,

the peace of the Son be ours this night,

the peace of the Father be ours this night,

the peace of all peace be ours this night,

each morning and evening of our lives.

May fears of day recede,

may treasures of night draw near.

7

Nature's breath and eyes are clearest blue;

O purest God, gaze on me this night.

The blackbird's call is wild and free,

may my spirit become free this night.

The Earth prepares for nightfall,

filled with Nature's abundance.

May I too never fail

to rejoice in your abundance.

8

Guardian of the planets,

kindler of the stars,

I pass into the darkness

encompassed by you.

Spirit of Truth, look down

upon a world in thrall to lies and illusions.

Work in the darkness

to bring all things into light.

9

In the name of the God of wholeness,

in the name of Compassion's Son,

in the name of the healing Spirit,

tonight may we be one.

10

Still is the earth;

make still my body.

Still is the night;

make still my mind.

Still are the spheres;

make still my soul.

11

Have mercy, God of Love,

this night on a surfeited world

that fails to grasp your love.

Have mercy this night on the weak and broken,

on the hungry, the homeless,

and souls without hope.

Have mercy, God of Love,

on my forgetfulness, my complaisance,

and my carelessness.

Teach me to love

as you do.

12

O Trinity of Love,

You were with me at the sun's rising:

Be with me till the day's end.

You were with me at the world's beginning:

Be with me till the world's end.

You were with me at my life's shaping:

Be with me at my life's end.

13

As darkness falls,

God bless the air.

Help us not to spoil it.

God bless the sea.

Help us not to poison it.

God bless the Earth.

Help us not to trample it.

God bless the planet.

Help us not to ruin it.

God bless here.

Help us look after it.

14

At the drawing in of the day,

may contemplation bring me peace.

May the soft mists of God's presence

wrap me in their gentle folds.

May the light of God's presence lengthen me.

May the might of God's presence strengthen me.

May the warmth of God's presence restore me.

May all that God has sowed in my life

flower and ripen.

May God's harvest in my life

be fruitful and abundant.

15

Blest be all creation
and all that has life.
Blest be the fire:
May it glow in me tonight.
Blest be the water:
May it bathe my being tonight.
Blest be the Earth:
May it uplift my bed tonight.
Blest be the air:
May it make my night breath sweet.

16

God to enfold me,

Christ to uphold me,

Spirit to inflame me,

this evening, always.

Father, Mother of us all,

as the day grows dim,

your name be hallowed.

Earth Mover, Pain Bearer, Giver of Life,

in your joy I end this day.

17

Risen Christ,

you burned in the hearts of two walkers

who made room in their conversation for you.

Burn in me as I converse with friends and family.

You revealed yourself to them

as they welcomed you into their home.

Reveal yourself to us

as we make a welcome in our home.

18

Shadows darken the day,
but the darkness shall not engulf me,
for with you, Christ, the darkness is light.
By your cross and precious death,
save me from the powers of evil.
Save me from another's harm;
save me from my selfish failings.
Come this night and give me calm.

19

All-knowing God, as this day ends,
teach me to pattern my life according to your ways;
forgive me for following idols and illusions.
All-seeing God, your prophets shine
like candles in the night;
forgive me if I closed my eyes today
to the light you wanted me to see.
All-holy God, frontrunners like John
clear obstacles from your path;
forgive me if I blocked your way today.
All-giving God, people like Mary offered their all
as bearers of your life;
help me too to be a bearer of your life.

20

Promised Spirit,

come as the evening dew,

come as the rain on dry land,

come as the fire in hours of cold,

come as a light lit in the dark.

Holy Spirit, come, renew my tired frame,

turn my deserts into pools of water,

renew in me your image of love.

BEDTIME

1

O angel guardian of my right hand,
attend to me this night.
Succor me, for I am feeble and forlorn;
steer my vessel in the tempests of my thoughts;
guide my mind in gap and in pit;
guard me in the treacherous turnings
and save me from thoughts that would destroy.
Save me from the harm I bring upon myself,
and protect me this night from a poisoned spirit;
O kindly angel of my right hand,
deliver me from all wickedness this night,
and may I sleep in peace.

2

Weaver of dreams,

weave well in me as I sleep.

Wisdom,

come into the storehouse of my memories,

be present though the silent hours,

and bring me safely to your glorious light.

3

May heaven's peacekeepers

encircle me all with their outstretched arms

to protect me from the hostile powers,

to put balm into my dreams,

to give me contented, sweet repose.

4

I lie down in peace,

knowing my sins are forgiven;

I lie down in peace,

knowing death has no threat.

I lie down in peace,

knowing no powers can harm me;

I lie down in peace,

knowing Jesus is near.

5

O Christ, Child of the living God,
may your holy angels guard my sleep.
May they watch over me as I rest
and hover around my bed.
Let them reveal to me in my dreams
visions of your glorious truth.
May no fears or worries delay
my willing, prompt repose.

6

I lie down this night with God,

and God will lie down with me;

I lie down this night with Christ,

and Christ will lie down with me;

I lie down this night with the Spirit,

and the Spirit will lie down with me;

God and Christ and the Spirit,

lying down with me.

7

The almighty and merciful Three circle me,
that asleep I may rest in peace.
As the Earth grows quiet in the dark,
may I quiet my heart with you.
Into your hands I place my failings and irritations.
In your presence, I give thanks
for the blessings of this day.
I will lie down at one with you
that I may rise up ready to do your will.

8

I place our souls and bodies
under your guarding this night, O God,
O kind Helper of frail pilgrims,
Protector of heaven and earth.
I place our souls and bodies
under your guiding this night, O Christ,
O Son of the tears and the woundings,
may your cross this night be our shield.
O gentle Companion and soul Friend,
our hearts' eternal Warmth,
I place our souls and bodies, O Spirit
under your glowing this night.

9

Lord Jesus Christ, who at this hour lay in the tomb
and so hallowed the grave to be a bed of hope,
may I lie down in hope and rise up with you.
I will no longer fear death,
for by your death you have destroyed death.
I will not lie down in anger,
for love has triumphed over hate.
I will not sleep as those without hope,
for by your rising you bring hope and life eternal.

10

Guardian, Source of Order,

Protect me through the hours of dark.

Take the restless maelstrom of my waking life

and as once you did with the cosmos,

create order out of chaos.

And then be pleased with me,

as you were pleased with your creation,

for I am your creation too.

11

This night, O Victor over death,
raise me from the death of denial;
raise me from the death of fear;
raise me from the death of despair.

This night, O Victor over death,
wake me to the eternal "Yes";
wake me to the rays of hope;
wake me to the light of dawn.

12

You fell asleep in mortal flesh, O Christ,

but on the third day you rose again.

Now you watch over me as I sleep;

you restore my soul and preserve my life.

In love of you I will take my rest.

Renew me this night, O Christ,

in body and soul,

that waking or sleeping

I may know your presence with me

13

Great God,

as you brought Jesus

safely through the night of sin and death

to his rising at dawn,

so bring me through this night

that I may offer you my prayers at dawn

and walk in light eternal.

14

Protect us through the hours of this night,

be they silent or stormy,

that we who are wearied

by the changes and chances of a restless world

may rest upon you eternally.

Come, Guardian of heaven and earth,

and cover me with night.

Night comes with the cold.

Night comes with the breath of death.

Night comes, the end comes, you come,

and your mercy is deeper than the night.

15

Great Spirit, who broods over the sleeping world,

as I sleep this night,

restore the garment of my self-respect

and remake me in your beauty.

Renew in me as I sleep

the stillness of my being,

the soundness of my body,

and bring to dawn my wholeness.

16

On your world, Life-Giver,
your love descend this night.
On your followers, Life-Giver,
your love descend this night.
On all who work throughout
the night hours, Life-Giver
your love descend this night
Where there is strife, Great Giver of Life,
your love descend this night.
Where there is neglect, Holy Giver of Life,
your love descend this night.
On all who sleep, Giver of Peace,
your love descend this night.

17

The day's troubles are over,
the fever of life has calmed,
and my work is done.
As I lay down my clothes,
may I lay down my struggles
before I go to sleep.
Now, Spirit, in your mercy,
give me a holy rest and peace
that I may awake refreshed.

18

O Christ who at this evening
hour rested in the tomb
and made it become a bed of hope,
visit this house tonight
that we may pass through the death of sleep
and rise from our beds in hope of life eternal.

19

I wait in the darkness expectantly, longingly.
Only in the darkness may I see
the splendor of the universe and the glowing stars.
In the darkness the wise three
saw the star that led them to the Christ Child.
In the darkness, God gave dreams
to Joseph and the wise three.
In the darkness of sleep, as dreams rise up,
open my mind to your messages.
For I know, Creator,
there is treasure in the darkness.
As it was in the dark vitality of the womb,
so may it be in the hidden life of my sleep.

20

I know that night is not dark with you,
O Giver of Life;
but a great deal of me is not yet one with you.
In the night the things I fear come to the surface.
The unacknowledged parts of my self
poke through the shadows to haunt me.
Night has a purpose of its own.
My task is to acknowledge the shadows
and bring them to you, the Morning Star.
You are author of light and dark.
The morning star would be nothing to us
without its prelude, the night.
So thank you, Lord, for the night.

IN THE MIDDLE OF THE NIGHT

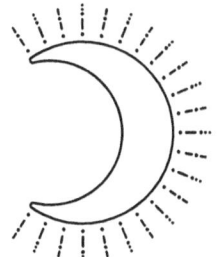

(in times of insomnia)

Repeat between ten and one hundred times:

Lord, have mercy on me.

*If you're not asleep by now,
you will be before you've finished saying what comes next.*

Repeat between ten and one hundred times:

I will lie down with God,
and God will lie down with me.

Sweet dreams!

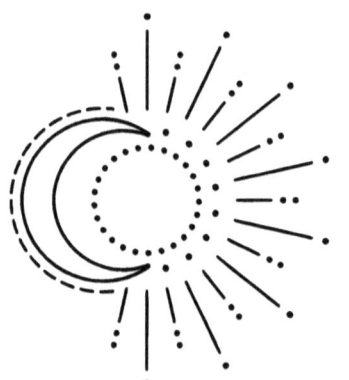

More books on Celtic spirituality that are also by Ray Simpson...

(All are available from Anamchara Books, Amazon, and most online booksellers.)

Celtic Book of Days

Ancient Wisdom for Each Day of the Year from the Celtic Followers of Christ

The ancient Celts found God's presence in each ordinary moment of the day. Everything they encountered revealed to them the presence of the sacred; each day was deep with meaning. Now you too can practice the Celts' faith, as you take a few moments to immerse yourself in their wisdom. These small daily moments of reflection and insight will open your heart to each day and all it holds.

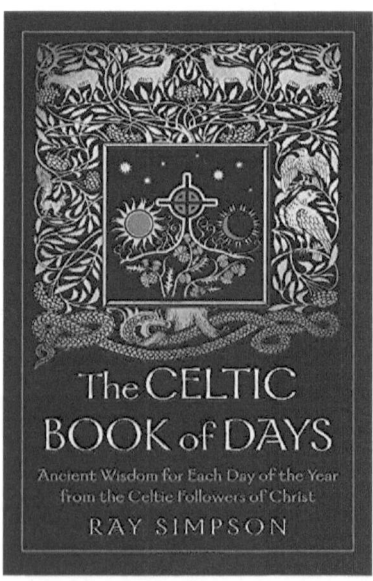

This day I call to me

> God's strength
> to direct me,
>
> God's power
> to sustain me,
>
> God's wisdom
> to guide me. . . .
>
> God's sheild
> to protect me.
>
> (Saint Patrick)

Celtic Christianity
Deep Roots for a Modern Faith

The world of the long-ago Celts appeals to many of us in the twenty-first century. Whether we are looking to find our cultural heritage or are seeking an alternative to worn and restrictive religious forms, the earth-centered, woman-friendly, inclusive faith of the Christian Celts offers us a deep-rooted alternative approach to traditional Christianity. The Celts experienced "thin places," where they sensed the supernatural world; they honored their poets, singers, and artists; and they passionately followed the Christ of the Gospels. Theirs was a church without walls, which lived naturally and comfortably within the community. Ray Simpson has spent most of his life walking in the footsteps of the Christian Celts, and now he allows us to experience for ourselves their dynamic spirituality.

Tree of Life
Celtic Prayers to the Universal Christ

Like a vast, ever-growing Tree of Life, Christ—the expression of Divine love—expands endlessly throughout the universe. This is the perspective of ancient Celtic spirituality, and it is this concept that Ray Simpson reveals in his poem-prayers. Inspired by the traditional Celtic style of prayer, he gives words to our individual relationships with God. He speaks of the wonder, beauty, and love revealed through the Universal Christ, the Tree of Life that includes all that is. Each and everything in creation is sacred, for everything is a word of God—and we too are called to be God's words to our world.

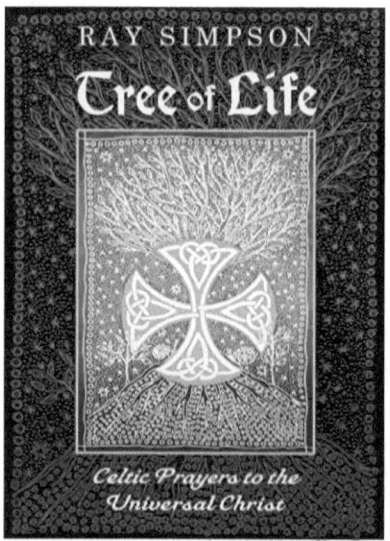

Soul Friendship in the Celtic Tradition
Ancient Insights for Today

The special friend who accompanies a person through life's journey is more precious than gold. The early Christian Celts had a heartwarming name for this person: the Anamchara. (Anam is the Gaelic word for soul; chara is the word for friend—"friend of the soul.") This special friend was someone with whom a person could talk through practical matters, reveal hidden intimacies, and break through the barriers of convention and egotism to an eternal unity of soul.

Ray Simpson brings this ancient concept into the twenty-first century, drawing practical applications from the long history of soul friendship. He describes a spiritual bond that lasts beyond this life into eternity, for it flows directly from God, who is the pattern of all friendship, the center and source of all human relationships.

AnamcharaBooks.com

www.ingramcontent.com/pod-product-compliance
Lightning Source LLC
Chambersburg PA
CBHW060527080526
44586CB00012B/650